Cricket

Heather L. Miller

KIDHAVEN PRESS™

THOMSON

GALE

San Diego • Detroit • New York • San Francisco • Cleveland
New Haven, Conn. • Waterville, Maine • London • Munich

For more information, contact
KidHaven Press
27500 Drake Rd.
Farmington Hills, MI 48331-3535
Or you can visit our Internet site at http://www.gale.com

LIBRARY OF CONGRESS CATALOGING-IN-PUBLICATION DATA
Miller, Heather.L.
Cricket / by Heather L. Miller.
p. cm. — (Bugs)
Includes bibliographical references and index.
Summary: Describes the physical characteristics of crickets, their life cycle, where they live, and their eating habits.
ISBN 0-7377-1768-8 (hardback : alk. paper)
1. Crickets—Juvenile literature. [1. Crickets.] I. Title. II.Series.
QL508.G8M56 2004
595.7'26—dc22
2003017750

Printed in China

CONTENTS

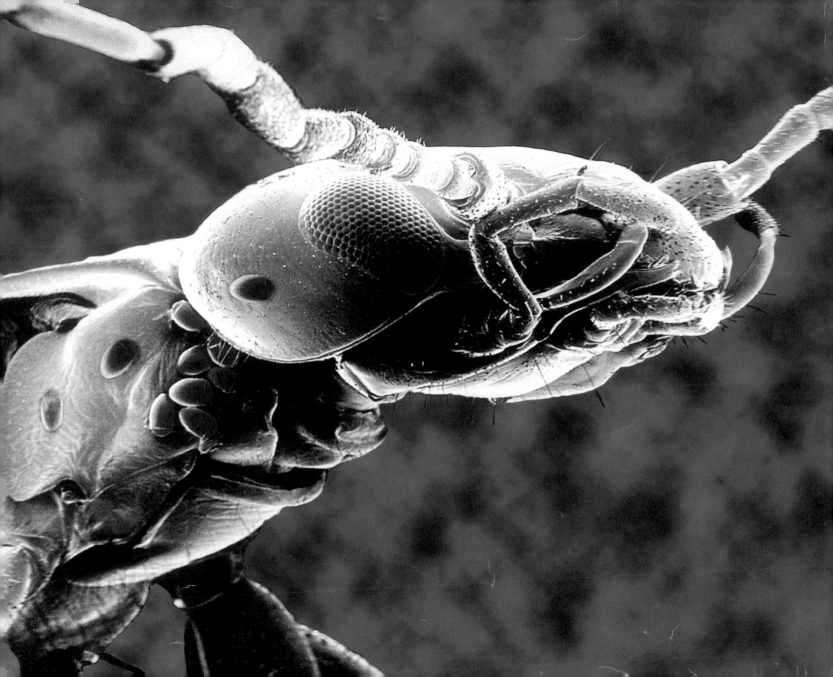

Meet the Cricket

Approximately one thousand different cricket species can be found hopping through forests, grasslands, beaches, and deserts in almost every country of the world. The light brown house cricket is a common cricket of Europe. The slightly larger field cricket is the most abundant cricket in the United States.

At about one inch long, house and field crickets are considered to be average-sized crickets. The

Opposite: Nearly one thousand different kinds of crickets live in the world. At left, a cricket head has been magnified many times its normal size.

5

largest cricket of all is the king cricket of Australia. At six inches long, this cricket is about the size of a hotdog. The ant-loving cricket is much smaller. The ant-loving cricket is so tiny it could rest on a sesame seed.

Cricket Parts

Whether large or small, all crickets are made up of the same three body sections—the **head, thorax,** and **abdomen**. The front section of the cricket is the head. Two antennae grow out from the top of the cricket's head. In some species these long, swooping appendages grow longer than the cricket's entire body. The cricket uses its antennae to discover how things feel and smell.

Along with the antennae, the cricket's head holds five eyes. Two **compound eyes** help the cricket sense movement. Each compound eye is made up of thousands of lenses. Each lens works independently, allowing the cricket to look in many different directions at the same time. With one compound eye on each side of the cricket's head, the cricket can sense

Crickets use their long antennae to feel and smell.

almost every movement that occurs in front of, behind, beside, or above itself.

Although the cricket's compound eyes are very specialized, they do not help the cricket sense the difference between light and dark. To determine whether it is day or night, the cricket must rely on its three **simple eyes**. Loaded with eyes and antennae, the cricket's head serves as a center for gathering information.

The body section attached to the cricket's head is called the thorax. The thorax provides an anchor for the cricket's wings and legs. Most crickets grow two sets of wings. Many crickets have wings so short they cannot be used for flight.

Power Jumper

Six legs grow out from under the wings of the cricket. The first four legs are short and thin. These legs are used for crawling and for grasping food. Two other long,

The king cricket of Australia is the world's largest cricket, growing up to six inches in length.

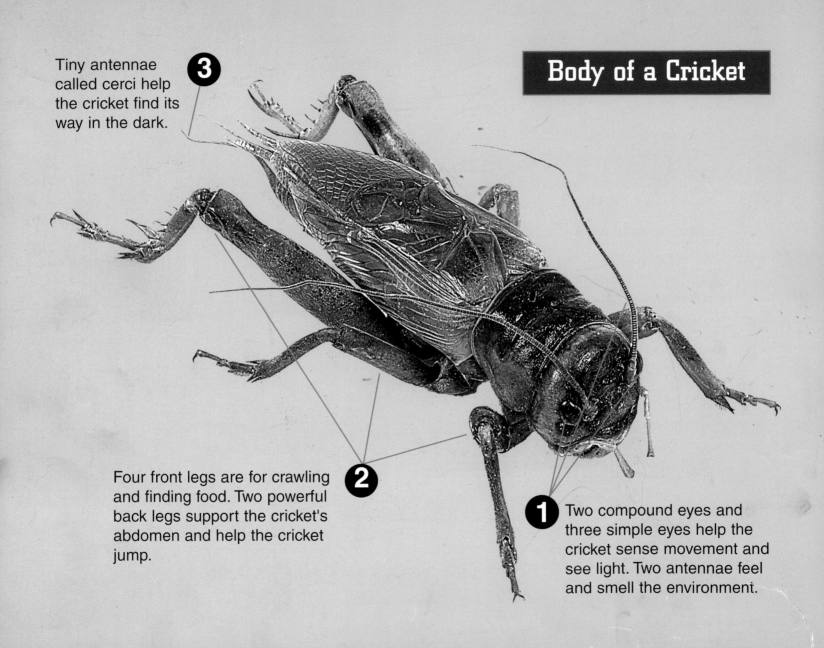

Body of a Cricket

Tiny antennae called cerci help the cricket find its way in the dark. **3**

Four front legs are for crawling and finding food. Two powerful back legs support the cricket's abdomen and help the cricket jump. **2**

1 Two compound eyes and three simple eyes help the cricket sense movement and see light. Two antennae feel and smell the environment.

strong legs are made specifically for jumping. Most crickets can jump two to three feet high. That is about twenty to thirty times more than their body length. If a four-foot-tall child could jump the same way, he or she could easily hop over an eight-story building.

Strong legs are also necessary for the cricket to carry its heavy back section. The abdomen, shaped like a long football, houses the cricket's gut, lungs, and other organs. The sides of the abdomen are lined with a series of tiny holes. The cricket uses these holes, called **spiracles**, to gather oxygen.

Rear-End Sensors

Just past the spiracles, at the very end of the cricket's body, are two spikelike antennae called **cerci**. Scientists believe the cricket uses the cerci to help find its way in the dark or while moving backward.

Fitted from front to back with sensory organs, the cricket is one insect that is well designed to investigate its surroundings.

Crickets use their strong legs to jump up to three feet in the air.

The Life Cycle

Opposite: The female cricket finds her mate by following the male's chirping.

The cricket's chirp is an important form of communication. In many species, only the male cricket is able to play the song that is so important in keeping the cricket population growing. During mating season, the male cricket uses his chirp to lure females.

The cricket produces its chirp by rubbing the edges of its two front wings together. Each of the cricket's front wings has a different edge. One wing has a sharp, smooth edge, while the other wing is lined with a series of tiny, toothlike ridges. When the male rubs the two edges together, the wings vibrate, creating a high-pitched pulse.

Finding a Female

A female cricket picks up the sounds through the ears on its legs. Just below the cricket's knees, a thin **tympanic membrane** gathers sound waves. The tympanic membrane vibrates and sends a message to the cricket's brain where it is interpreted as a mating call.

If the female considers the call to be from a suitable mate, she will hop toward the sound until she finds the chirping male. When the female cricket arrives, the male often changes his mating call to a courtship song. Soon after they meet, mating occurs.

Hiding the Eggs

After mating, eggs begin to develop inside the female cricket. When the eggs are ready, the

The female cricket's tympanic membrane (above), located just below her knees, picks up the chirping of males during the mating season.

female uses a long, needlelike tube, called an **ovipositor,** to insert them into a safe place.

Each species of cricket chooses to lay their eggs in a different place. Many tree crickets lay their eggs in tree branches or plant stems. Under a magnifying glass, tiny, pin-sized holes, lined in perfect rows, can be seen on tree branches after the snowy tree cricket lays her eggs. Some cave crickets and camel crickets lay their eggs in bat dung, or guano, while the field cricket tends to lay its eggs underground.

A ground cricket lays her eggs on the stem of a prickly thorn bush.

Breaking Out

After the eggs rest for fifteen to twenty-five days, young crickets begin to emerge. In some species, new crickets are equipped with a small "egg tooth" that they use to tear out of their shells.

A newly hatched cricket is called a **pronymph.** A pronymph has no legs, wings, or antennae. After a few minutes of wiggling,

A cricket nymph sheds its outer shell, or exoskeleton, up to twelve times before emerging as an adult.

the pronymph will undergo its first **molt**. The pronymph's outer shell, or **exoskeleton**, splits and a larger, more mature **nymph** crawls out.

Nymphs are small but look very similar to adult crickets. Nymphs are usually lighter in color than full-grown crickets, and they do not have wings. Nymphs molt about twelve times before they are fully developed. Most reach a mature state within a year.

Deep Freeze

After growing for several months, the adult cricket is ready to reproduce. Depending on where the cricket lives, winter may be only weeks away by the time the female is mature enough to deposit her eggs.

While her eggs can survive the harsh temperatures of winter, the adult female cannot. The expected life span of a

cricket is about one year. Unless it can find warm shelter, the cricket will most likely die in the freezing temperatures of winter. As the warmth of spring returns, new pronymphs will emerge from their eggs, and the life cycle of the cricket will begin again.

Young crickets like this one emerge in the spring and begin to search for a mate.

Cricket Homes

Crickets can be found living in many places. Some crickets live aboveground, others live on the ground, and a few species live underground.

As their names suggest, tree crickets and bush crickets live aboveground, where they find shelter in the branches of trees and bushes. Many tree crickets feel comfortable between the leaves of almost any tree, but some crickets choose to make their homes in certain types of trees. Pine trees provide the only suitable shelter for the pine cricket. The black-horned tree cricket is often found in raspberry bushes. The oak bush cricket crawls up tall tree trunks.

Field crickets and house crickets find shelter close to the ground. These crickets can sometimes be found hopping through backyards. Their chirps can be heard coming from dark corners of basements and garages. The field cricket is most commonly found in damp places such as riverbeds and moist grasslands. It often builds shallow tunnels in the soft soil where it hides during the day.

The leaflike appearance of the green bush cricket allows the insect to live unseen by predators.

Living Underground

While the field cricket may hide underground, the mole cricket spends most of its life beneath the soil. The mole cricket is equipped with strong front legs, which it uses to dig a series of tunnels. The tunnels a mole cricket digs can sometimes be seen aboveground. Small, meandering trails of pushed-up soil resemble those made by a garden mole.

Along with building tunnels, the mole cricket digs other special features when constructing its burrow. A typical mole cricket burrow has one or more living chambers as well as a chamber for holding waste. The entrance to a mole cricket's burrow serves a specific purpose. The mole cricket builds a funnel-shaped entrance, which acts as a megaphone. The unique design amplifies the cricket's chirp so that it can be heard more than one mile away. When the mole cricket does not want to be heard, it seals the entrance of its burrow with leaves and mud.

Other types of crickets also live underground. The camel cricket lives underground but does not build a burrow. Unable to move in bright light, the

Hundreds of crickets, like this king cricket, cover the side of a building. Crickets live in many different habitats.

The camel cricket (right) lives in dark places like caves and sewers, while the black-horned tree cricket (below) makes its home in tall trees.

camel cricket chooses to live in damp, dark spaces such as caves, basements, and sewers. The smallest of all crickets also prefers to live in the dark. The ant-loving cricket makes its home in underground ant nests, where it becomes part of the ant community.

Depending on its species, the cricket can be found living above the ground in trees, on the ground within the grasses, or underground in burrows. The cricket is an adaptive insect that has found many ways to create the perfect home.

Eating Machine

The cricket is an omnivore, which means it eats both plant and animal material. The list of items on a cricket's menu is almost endless. The cricket is known to eat dead insects, old clothing, fungi, seeds, leather, paper, glue from book bindings and wallpaper, fruits, vegetables, meat, and even other crickets.

Although the cricket may seem to have an appetite for just about anything, different species of crickets do

have special tastes. Tree crickets, such as the oak bush cricket, tend to show a preference for aphids and leaves. Underground crickets, such as the mole cricket, chew on the roots of plants, earthworms, and larvae.

Another underground cricket, the ant-loving cricket, feeds on the waxy substances secreted by the ants it lives with. These crickets are also believed to feed on newly hatched ants.

Incredible Jaws

Two pairs of strong jaws make devouring a wide range of foods an easy job for the cricket. The **mandibles** are the first set of jaws found in a cricket's mouth. These jaws have sharp, jagged edges and are used to cut up and grind food. The second set of jaws, found behind the mandibles, are called the **maxillae**. These jaws are covered by a few small teeth and are used to rake food into the cricket's mouth.

Two **palps** extend out from the maxillae. The cricket uses its palps to feel and taste food. The palps are especially useful for finding food at night when the cricket does most of its feeding.

Opposite: A hungry house cricket eats a flower. Crickets eat both plant and animal material.

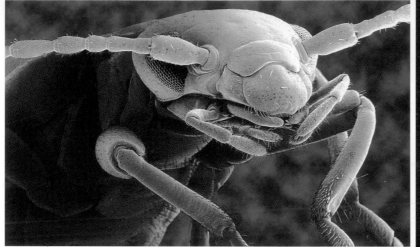

The cricket uses its two sets of jaws, known as the mandibles and maxillae (shown above), to cut and chew food (right).

While the cricket may be a busy eater during the night, it is a prime target for predators during the day. The list of creatures that prey on crickets is long. Birds, mice, moles, weasels, snakes, lizards, beetles, wasps, and spiders all consider the cricket to be a tasty meal.

Crickets Undercover

Because they are so heavily hunted, most crickets have come up with clever ways to hide. The giant bush cricket's green color helps it blend in with the leaves of trees and bushes, making it very difficult for predators to find. The stone cricket, found in the Namaqualand Desert of South Africa, is an expert at camouflage. This cricket looks just like a small, white rock. Even the stone cricket's eyes are white, making it nearly impossible to spot on the desert floor.

Despite the cricket's elaborate efforts to stay out of sight, it often finds itself under attack. The cricket's first line of defense is to hop away. If a predator is lucky enough to catch the cricket in midair, it may end up with an unexpected surprise. The cricket's legs detach easily, allowing the cricket to escape, leaving a single leg behind in the predator's mouth.

Stinky Spray

Some crickets have developed a method of defense

An orb spider weaves a web around a cricket before eating the insect.

A hungry frog approaches an unsuspecting cricket. Although crickets have many enemies, they are very successful insects.

even more creative than dropping a leg. When in danger, many crickets are able to spit up their stomach contents, making themselves taste bad to predators. The king cricket has learned that tasting bad is not the only way to get rid of unwanted visitors. By spraying its own fecal matter, the king cricket produces an odor that is extremely offensive to many predators.

The cricket is a hearty eater that has many enemies. The cricket's cheerful chirps provide proof that even though it is heavily hunted, it is an abundant and successful insect.

GLOSSARY

abdomen: Large, rear section of a cricket.

cerci: Set of spikelike antennae located at the rear of the cricket.

compound eye: An eye made up of many tiny lenses.

exoskeleton: Outer protective shell covering the cricket's body.

head: Front section of a cricket's body.

mandibles: Outermost set of jaws used to cut and grind food.

maxillae: Inner set of jaws used to pull food into the mouth.

molt: To shed an outer shell or covering.

nymph: Young cricket that closely resembles an adult.

ovipositor: Long, tubelike organ used to deposit eggs.

palps: Segmented, tactile mouthpart.

pronymph: Newly hatched cricket with no legs, wings, or antennae. Stage prior to nymph.

simple eyes: Eyes that sense light and dark.

spiracles: Holes through which a cricket gathers air.

thorax: Midsection of cricket. It serves as an anchor for legs and wings.

tympanic membrane: Thin tissue that receives sound waves.

FOR FURTHER EXPLORATION

Books

Melvin Berger, *Chirping Crickets*. New York: HarperCollins Children's Books, 1998. This book gives understandable explanations on how to tell the temperature by listening to cricket chirps. It also provides ideas for fun, cricket-related activities.

Cari Meister, *Crickets*. Edina, MN: ABDO, 2002. Part of the Checkerboard Science and Nature Library, *Crickets*, tells about what crickets eat, where they live, and how they relate to humans.

Elaine Pascoe, *Nature's Close-Up Crickets and Grasshoppers*. Wood-bridge, CT: Blackbirch Press, 1999. Excellent photographs reinforce many interesting facts about grasshoppers and crickets. A special section tells how to gather and keep crickets as pets.

Websites

Enchanted Learning (www.enchanted learning.com). Search for crickets and find a printable diagram showing the body parts of the cricket.

Singing Insects of North America (http://buzz.ifas.ufl.edu). Click on the link below the table of contents to find a large selection of sounds and drawings of singing insects. Turn up the volume on your computer, and listen to the songs of crickets.

Tree of Life Web Project (www. tolweb.org). This website offers helpful links as well as sophisticated information and photographs detailing a variety of crickets.

INDEX

PICTURE CREDITS

ABOUT THE AUTHOR

Heather L. Miller has written more than twenty books for young readers as well as a wide range of educational materials for elementary grade teachers. Ms. Miller lives in Indiana with her husband and two daughters, where she enjoys camping and listening to the crickets chirp during the night.